# Contents

# What is wind?

Wind is air that moves.

You cannot see wind.

But you can feel the wind
on your skin. You can hear
it blowing leaves on trees.

# How do we use wind?

Wind helps some boats to move. The wind blows on the **sails**. This pushes the boat along.

whatever the weather

# WIND

Lauren Taylor

QED

Editor: Alexandra Koken
Designer: Melissa Alaverdy
Educational consultants:
  Jillian Harker and
  Heather Adamson

Copyright © QED Publishing 2013

First published in the UK in 2013
by QED Publishing
A Quarto Group Company
230 City Road,
London EC1V 2TT

www.qed-publishing.co.uk

ISBN 978 1 78171 223 8

A catalogue record
for this book is
available from
the British Library.

Printed in China

Words in **bold**
can be found in
the Glossary on
page 24.

We also use wind to make **power** for our homes.

# Feel the breeze

A light wind is called a **breeze**. A breeze can keep you cool on a warm day.

# Gale

A very strong wind is called a **gale.**

Gales can snap tree branches.
They can even blow down old trees.

# Hurricanes and tornadoes

We call the strongest wind a **hurricane** or **tornado**. A hurricane is strong enough to blow down a house.

A tornado is a
swirling wind that
hangs down from
a storm cloud.

# Wind and plants

Some plants use
wind to
scatter
their **seeds**.

The wind blows on the plant. It carries the seeds. They land on new **soil** where they can grow.

# Making waves

The wind makes waves in the sea. Waves make boats bob up and down.

Gales can make very big waves.

# On the wing

Animals also use the
wind. Birds use the
wind to help them fly.

Some birds can **glide** on the wind. They fly without flapping their wings for a long time.

# What to wear

Strong winds can
blow your hair
around. You can
wear a hat to
keep it in place.

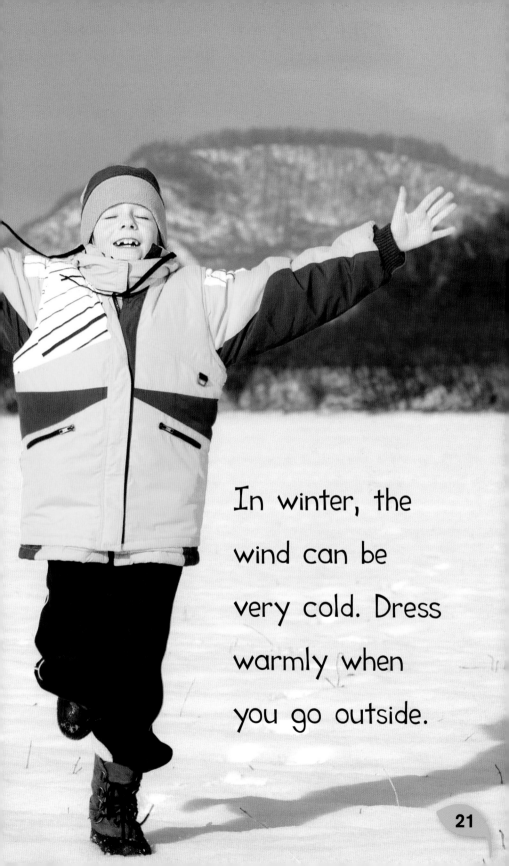

In winter, the wind can be very cold. Dress warmly when you go outside.

# Windy weather fun

You can go to the top of a hill to fly a kite in the wind.

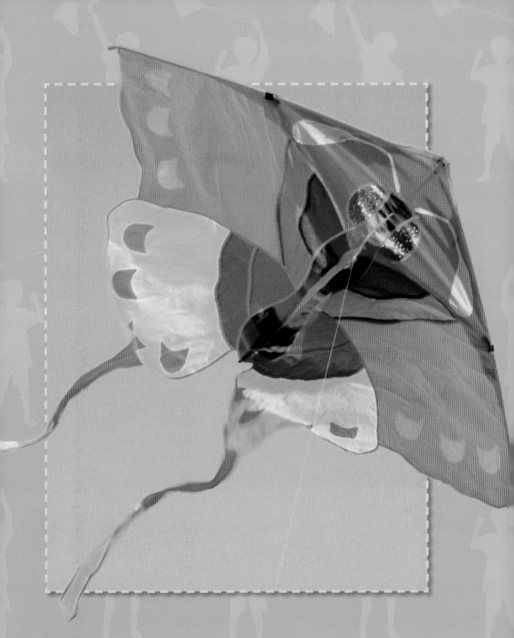

The wind is stronger up
high. This helps your kite
to lift into the air.

# Glossary

**breeze** a light wind

**gale** a very strong wind

**glide** to fly without power

**hurricane** a violent storm with heavy rain and high winds

**power** electricity or other forms of energy

**sail** a large piece of canvas that moves a boat by catching the wind

**seed** the part of a flowering plant from which a new plant can grow

**soil** the top layer of dirt, where plants grow

**tornado** a violent windstorm that appears as a dark funnel hanging down from a cloud